The Gift Of You

By Michelle Lepitre

Expanded Edition

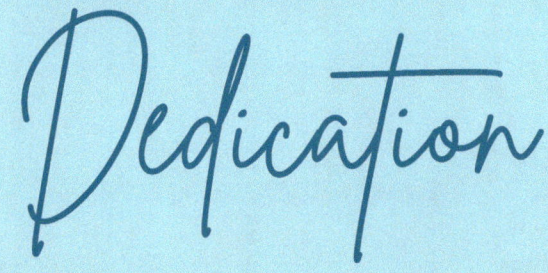

Dedication

"For all the hearts that grow through love and kindness. This is a true story of how love, friendship, faith, and God's blessings brought our family together. Dedicated to Briana, our beloved Aunt Bebe, my wonderful husband, and above all, to God, whose love made this journey possible."

Love,
Michelle

The Gift Of You

By Michelle Lepitre
Expanded Edition

Once upon a time, Mommy and Daddy dreamed of you. They imagined your bright smile, your curious eyes, and the kindness in your heart. But no matter how much they dreamed, Mommy's tummy wasn't able to carry a baby. Year after year, they held onto hope, waiting for the day their dream would come true.

One day, Mommy and Daddy's best friend, Aunt Bebe, said something wonderful. She said, "I have a big heart and a strong tummy. I'd love to carry a baby for you!"

Mommy and Daddy were overjoyed! They hugged Aunt Bebe tightly, their hearts were overflowing with gratitude.

She was giving them the most precious gift of all—the gift of helping bring you into the world.

Before long, Aunt Bebe's tummy began to grow, and we knew you were on your way. Mommy and Daddy read you a special story filled with love and hope. They recorded it so you could hear their voices and feel their love even before you were born.

Aunt Bebe played the story for you every day. She placed soft headphones on her belly so you could hear Mommy and Daddy's voices as they read to you, telling you how much they loved you even before you were born.

When you were ready, the big day came! Aunt Bebe gave you to Mommy and Daddy, and their hearts were so full of love, they could hardly speak. You were their greatest dream come true.

Families are made in many different ways, but each one is built with love. God brought Aunt Bebe into Mommy's life as a dear friend, and her gift helped bring you into the world.

You were created out of extraordinary love, and God's blessings have been with us every step of the way.

"For I know the plans I have for you," declares the Lord, "plans to prosper you and not to harm you, plans to give you hope and a future." — Jeremiah 29:11

A Closing Note from Mommy and Daddy

My Sweet Boy,

This story is the story of how you came into our lives. It is a story of love, faith, and hope. We want you to know that from the very beginning, you were surrounded by love—from Aunt Bebe's generous heart to the many prayers we lifted for you. You are our greatest blessing, and we thank God for you every single day.

Remember, you were chosen, cherished, and celebrated even before you were born. You are a part of God's perfect plan, and we are so grateful to be your Mommy and Daddy.

With all our love,

Mommy & Daddy.

MICHELLE

LEPITRE

About the Author

Michelle Lepitre is a faith-driven wife, mom, and former educator. With a background in special education and Applied Behavior Analysis, she dedicates her time to writing and creating faith-inspired content. She finds joy in sharing heartfelt stories that celebrate love, family, and God's blessings, hoping to inspire faith and connection in every reader.

www.ingramcontent.com/pod-product-compliance
Lightning Source LLC
LaVergne TN
LVHW071701060526
838201LV00038B/403